Taking Pictures

Taking
Pictures

by Nina Leen

Holt, Rinehart and Winston
New York

To the young photographers, Stacey, Audra, Kellie, and Timothy, many thanks for their cooperation.
I am also grateful for the help the Quogue Elementary School in Long Island, New York, gave me.

10 9 8 7 6 5 4 3 2 1

Library of Congress Cataloging in Publication Data

Leen, Nina
  Taking pictures.
  SUMMARY: A guide for the young child in operating
a camera, with suggestions for photographing animals and for
making backgrounds for indoor shots.
  1. Photography—Juvenile literature.
[1. Photography] I. Title.
TR149.L43   770'.28   76-41156
ISBN 0-03-018701-X

Contents

Note to Adults

Many people may not consider photography a project for five year olds. They think it's much too early. It is not. Pictures are the language understood by people all over the world. This is why it makes sense to let children learn about photography as early as possible. It teaches them to look around and discover their surroundings, to observe and tell with pictures more than they can describe with words. Their imagination is not yet burdened by technique; they learn to see and to react, to speak with pictures. The first camera should be simple, requiring little or no adjustment.

There are several cameras that are simple enough for a child to use. The cameras may look different, but they all have the same three parts in common: a viewfinder, a release button, and a film advance wheel. Most also have an attachment for flash. In all, the lens is "fixed focus"—meaning it is sharp for a distance of four or five feet to infinity.

New cameras are accompanied by an instruction sheet explaining how that particular camera works and how to load and unload the film. This instruction sheet is very important and should be carried with camera and film. It is a good idea to make a copy to have in case the original should be lost.

Note to the Young Photographer

First, get used to the camera. Practice with toys. They do not move. Also, they can be placed where light and background are right for taking a picture. Take the pictures outdoors in the daytime.

When you have some experience taking pictures of toys, you can photograph living models—friends and animals. Living models may move a little. But that is nothing to worry about. So long as the model does not move around, your picture is safe. Stay calm, and press the release button slowly and firmly.

Plan your picture because there are only twelve exposures in a roll of film. Don't snap pictures that nobody, including you, will want to look at.

The Camera

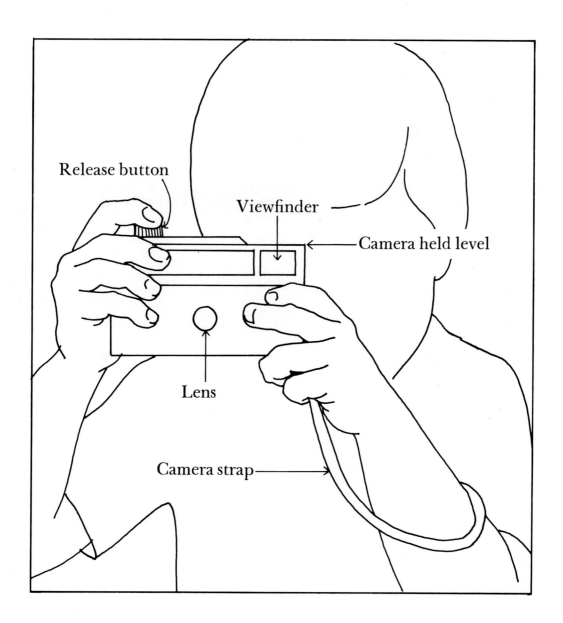

Release button

Viewfinder

Camera held level

Lens

Camera strap

Shooting the Picture

Distance

The distance between you and the toy dog should be at least four feet. This is the length of an average broom handle. The following exercise will help you guess distance. Look at the broom handle on the ground. Then go and stand about four feet away from a nonmoving object like a toy, a tree, or some steps. Check the distance with the broom handle.
Practice this. You will soon be guessing correctly without the aid of the broom handle.

11

Center the subject in the viewfinder

Look through the viewfinder.
The dog should be sitting in the center of the picture.

Keep fingers away from the lens

If you touch the lens, part of the picture
will be dark (unexposed) .

It will look like this.

Hold the camera level

If the camera is not held level, this will happen.

Your picture of the toy dog should look like this.

Taking Pictures Outdoors

Still Subjects

Toys are still objects.
They do not move.

Shadows can spoil a picture.
Do not place the toy bear
in the shadow of a tree.

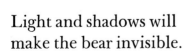

Light and shadows will
make the bear invisible.

The best place to take the bear's picture
is in direct light.

Invent a story

Call your story *The Adventures of Little Bear.*

The bear can climb a tree . . .

look over a fence . . .

or hide behind
a broom.
What other ideas
do you have?

Living Models

A cat, resting on the steps, is a nice picture
with a simple, uncluttered background.

After they eat, cats usually wash their paws and faces.
They don't move around much.
It's a good time to take their picture.

A dog will often pose for a picture
if the owner tells him to sit.

People are easy to photograph if they want to cooperate.
Ask your friend to hold a pet when you take the picture.

Unexpected pictures

You can never tell what you might see. . . .

A young bird has fallen out of its nest. It can't find the way back. It sits on the ground and hopes that its mother will come to feed it.

This squirrel has found something tasty. It pauses on the rim
of a wastebasket to eat. If you don't make sudden moves
to frighten it, you will be able to take its picture.

Patience

A wildlife refuge or zoo is a good place to practice photography. Many animals are outdoors, and there is no problem with the lighting. Do not take pictures of animals behind bars. Such pictures are never appealing. Also, it can be dangerous to hold the camera between the bars. Unexpectedly, some animal may reach out and grab the camera and the photographer. But there are many animals to choose from. All you need is patience. A photographer has to be patient. Make yourself comfortable. Sit on a bench, or lean against a tree. It may take time.

The little prairie dog is appealing.
Its favorite position is standing up and looking around.
They are called "dogs" because they utter a sound like a bark.

It's easy to take a picture of camels. They walk slowly.
They stop to look at people. A young camel usually walks
close to its mother. You can take a family portrait.

Here is something that might make a good subject.
A brown pelican rests at the edge of the water. If you have
patience . . .

. . . you will see him lift his wings, preparing for a swim.
Hold the camera firmly, and press the release button.
The long wait was worth it.

Stand on a small bridge or on high ground.
You might see a mallard duck swim by.

From his pool in the zoo,
a young seal might look up at your camera.

The giraffe is the tallest animal in the world.
In the zoo you can see its head high above the fence.

Hold up the camera.
Once you see the giraffe
in the viewfinder,
do not move the camera.

If the camera is moved
the giraffe's head
may be cut off.

The sun should be over the giraffe's head, not behind it.

Make Your Own Backgrounds

If you can't go out, draw a background for your toys. You need two white cardboards. Draw a background on one. You can use felt-tipped markers, crayons, chalk, or water colors. Stand the cardboard with the drawing against the wall, place the plain cardboard underneath, and put your toy on it. To photograph indoors, use a flash. If you take the picture outdoors, make sure there is no wind, or it will blow your toy and background away.

An African landscape is just right for a stuffed giraffe.

This is the setup.

This is the picture.

Mouse has a visitor

Draw a room with a black felt-tipped marker.
Put the toy mice in front and take the picture.

Bee between flowers

For the toy bee, paint a background of flowers.
Take her picture in the "garden" you have made for her.

Sailboat and Birds

On one sheet of soft blue or gray paper, draw waves
and birds with white chalk.
Bend the paper at the bottom and put a small sailboat on it.

Car in the city

For your car, draw a background of a city street.
You can use crayons and a ruler to draw the houses.

Taking Indoor Pictures

With flash

Whatever moves can have its picture taken indoors
with flash.
A playful kitten is a good subject.

When Spot brings you the old rubber, use flash
to take his picture.

With daylight

If your classroom has large windows and light colored walls,
on a bright day you can take a picture of your teacher.

If it's a sunny day, and you want to take a picture of your
sister, all dressed up, have her sit close to a window.
Be sure to lift the shade or curtains.

Take the Camera With You

After taking many outdoor pictures, you can start a collection of your own best photographs. When you go on a trip with your family to some interesting place like Marineland or an outdoor circus—take pictures. Don't be timid, by now you know the rules. You can do it.

The porpoise in Marineland is curious and playful.

In an outdoor circus, clowns don't mind posing for pictures.
They know that even their pictures make people laugh.